E. Ashley Rooney
WITH Jo Ann Alston

DÉCOR

Nursery

Schiffer
Publishing Ltd

4880 Lower Valley Road • Atglen, PA 19310

**Other Schiffer Books
on Related Subjects:**

Children's Rooms: From Newborn to Teens,
0-7643-2147-1, $24.95

*Kid's Decor: Interior Inspirations,
Infants through Teens,*
0-7643-1613-3, $24.95

Copyright © 2013
by E. Ashley Rooney

Library of Congress
Control Number: 2012953138

Designed by Justin Watkinson
Cover by Danielle Farmer
Type set in Scriptina/Adobe Song Std/
NewBskrvll BT/Humanst521 BT

ISBN: 978-0-7643-4301-8
Printed in China

Published by Schiffer Publishing, Ltd.
4880 Lower Valley Road
Atglen, PA 19310
Phone: (610) 593-1777
Fax: (610) 593-2002
E-mail: Info@schifferbooks.com

For the largest selection of fine reference books on this and related subjects, please visit our website at:
  www.schifferbooks.com.
You may also write for a free catalog.

This book may be purchased from the publisher.
Please try your bookstore first.

We are always looking for people to write books on new and related subjects. If you have an idea for a book, please contact us at:
proposals@schifferbooks.com.

Schiffer Books are available at special discounts for bulk purchases for sales promotions or premiums. Special editions, including personalized covers, corporate imprints, and excerpts can be created in large quantities for special needs. For more information contact the publisher.

In Europe, Schiffer books are distributed by
Bushwood Books
6 Marksbury Ave.
Kew Gardens
Surrey TW9 4JF England
Phone: 44 (0) 20 8392 8585
Fax: 44 (0) 20 8392 9876
E-mail: info@bushwoodbooks.co.uk
Website: www.bushwoodbooks.co.uk

COVER PHOTOS: Elisabeth Fall Photography, Stephen Michael Garey Photography, © Halkin Photography LLC, Jim Landers, Marco Ricca Photography. BACK COVER: Marco Ricca Photography, Jim Landers, and © Stanley Furniture Co. Young America.

ACKNOWLEDGMENTS

Acknowledgments

The creative act never ceases to amaze me; each new book is a novel experience, an adventure, and a challenge. There is a reason why I selected the designers for this book. They do classy work.

It was the work of designer Jo Ann Alston that triggered this book. I am delighted to include her insights here. She was joined by many other talented designers. Lilli Design provided some interesting presentation boards; my daughter-in-law, Ellie Lund, provided significant young mother information; and Barbara Purchia is a thoughtful editor.

Contents

From the moment you bring your baby home, his or her (or their!) room will become a special place for you and your child. Even if you keep your baby in your bedroom at night initially, you'll probably use the baby's room for changing diapers and other everyday tasks. The sooner you and your child feel that you belong in the nursery, the better.

When it comes to decorating the nursery, most parents select a theme. It can be gender neutral, such as farm animals in bright colors or nursery rhymes, or gender specific, such as toy soldiers or fairies. Some want a vintage design while others prefer educational. Of course, you can change the décor to suit your children as he, she, or they grow, but you may want to consider whether you plan to update it on a regular basis. Parents who choose a neutral color for the wall covering can simply add accessories and small decorations that can be changed and moved around as the child grows. Other parents change the theme and design every three to five years depending on their child's taste.

Sigrid Burnett created a bright blue nursery for her twin girls.

5

Almost any color scheme can work, but it's usually best to keep colors on the clear, light side. In the following pages, you'll see how light, cheerful tints such as mint green, yellow, and brilliant blues, combined with a variety of special accents, can look fresh and delightfully personal.

A general rule is that your nursery should be a fun room that will grow with your children. The furniture should be practical and safe and should include a comfortable rocking or easy chair for you to hold your baby. Safety and style are key here. You will need a crib that meets modern safety standards, a conventional changing table with a built-in rail and/or safety straps to prevent the baby from rolling off the table, and storage for clothes and toys.

In the Introduction, Jo Ann Alston, an ASID award-winning certified interior designer, describes the health, safety, and aesthetic considerations involved in decorating a nursery, and then many designers from throughout the United States will show you a variety of different designs for your baby's nursery, toddler room, and playroom.

Courtesy of CasaPosh and Jim Landers.

INTRODUCTION
DECORATING THE NURSERY

Decorating the Nursery

Jo Ann Alston, NJCID
Allied Member ASID - Principal
J. Stephens Interiors

Excitement, wonder, hopes, and dreams are just some of the feelings a prospective mother is feeling as she prepares for the birth of her baby. Many selections and preparations need to be made to welcome the baby home to a healthy, safe, and aesthetically pleasing nursery.

HEALTH

Researchers have discovered that prospective parents should consider how everything is made, what chemicals are in it, and how it can affect your baby. In investigating some of the important health issues facing a newborn, I turned to "Green" expert Patricia Gaylo, who points out that everything in the nursery can affect the health and welfare of the baby.

In designing your nursery, make sure it is safe and nontoxic. Founded in 2001, the GREENGUARD Environmental Institute (GEI)'s mission is to improve human health and quality of life by enhancing indoor air quality and reducing people's exposure to chemicals and other pollutants. In keeping with that mission, GEI certifies products and materials for low chemical emissions and provides a free resource for choosing healthier products and materials for indoor environments. Look for GEI-certified furniture and avoid pressed wood, particleboard and plywood, which can contain formaldehyde and, as a result, lead to health problems.

Gaylor recommends using a real wood floor since carpets can harbor dust mites. She urges that you purchase a wood floor made in the USA of substantially harvested wood from local merchants. Unfortunately, when you purchase materials from other countries you may get something other than what you wanted. In addition, be sure that no volatile organic compounds (VOCs) adhesive is used when your floor is laid. Since synthetic rugs will emit some VOCs, she suggests using cotton area rugs with no slip pads underneath them on the wood floors.

Courtesy of Greenguard
Environmental Institute.

Courtesy of Terra Cabinets.

You should also use a low or NO levels of VOC paint in the nursery. Most of the major paint manufacturers have low VOC paint. Mythic® paint is one supplier of no VOC paint. Sherwin Williams has a line of paints especially designed for use in baby's rooms. The firm has even designed specific color palettes, which give the customers a chance to comfortably blend two or more colors of paints together to create a desired look. The room should be painted one month before you bring the baby home. Expectant mothers should not be exposed to paint fumes, and the room should be well ventilated, for at least one month after painting.

Ventilating in the nursery is important. Your windows should open and should not be near the baby's furniture. They also should have a child lock or a window guard to protect the child since, as the child gets older, he/she may try crawling up and out! Of course, you will want to make sure you have a sturdy screen on the window. Use a cool-air humidifier instead of a vaporizer in the room. Clean it frequently and empty it when not in use. Archives of *Pediatrics and Adolescent Medicine* (October 2008) reported that a ceiling fan dramatically reduced the chance of sudden infant death syndrome (SIDs) by seventy-two percent.

Gaylor also recommends real wooden blinds rather than plastic, which can leach chemicals into the air. Cords are a major strangulation risk. To keep cords out of reach of children use cord locks. You could also use a cordless cellular shade. These treatments should be vacuumed on regular basis. Using a HEPA Filter Vacuum traps dust mites and allergens from carpets and furniture.

Finally, Gaylor suggests Terra cabinets for closet materials. The firm uses SkyBlend™ (particleboard that emits very low levels of formaldehyde) and Columbia Forest Products' UV cured interior plywood that contains a formaldehyde free resin ("FFR Plywood").

An organic formaldehyde-free mattress is another key component. Regular mattresses are treated with a chemical fire retardant (PBDEs) that can ultimately impact our endocrine and nervous systems. Organic mattresses use carbon as a natural fire retardant. CleanBrands manufactures and distributes a line of hypoallergenic products, including pillow and mattress casements, stuffed pillows, and window treatments. Gaylor recommends that you use one hundred percent organic cotton sheets and pillows, as these won't affect the baby's sensitive skin. The sheets should fit snugly so as to prevent a child from getting wrapped up in a sheet. She also recommends not using a pillow until your baby is a toddler.

Crib bumper pads are a common baby product, and parents often use them thinking they are increasing the safety of their child's crib. However, many health agencies now recommend that parents do not use them. They believe the need for crib bumpers has passed and that their use may actually put children at greater risk for suffocation or SIDS.

One line of furniture that is GREENGUARD Certified is the moderately priced Stanley Young America Collection, made in North Carolina. This practical collection offers a crib that converts to a single bed for later use. © by Stanley Furniture Co. *Courtesy of Young America.*

SAFETY

Designing your dream nursery is more than design aesthetics and cute furniture. Of course, the aesthetics and furniture are the fun part, but there's also the safety part. Home accidents send nearly two million children under the age of four to the emergency room every year, according to Safe Kids Worldwide. So before your new baby moves in, use these tips to inspect the big potential trouble spots in your nursery.

- Place a smoke and carbon monoxide detector in or near your child's bedroom.
- Use plug protectors in all electrical outlets.
- Use childproof locks on cupboards containing dangerous substances.

The Crib

Any crib for sale in a store must comply with current Federal regulations. Health and safety problems can occur when you use an older crib.

The slats shouldn't be more than 2-3/8" apart so your baby can't get her head stuck in them. Cutout designs on the end panels are also dangerous. Check out the corner posts too: they shouldn't have any decorative knobs or other elements on top that could snag your baby's clothing and lead to strangulation or other serious injuries. Check (and regularly recheck) the screws, bolts, and mattress supports to make sure they're not loose or broken. Always lock the side rail in its raised position whenever you place your child in the crib. As soon as your child can stand up, adjust the mattress to its lowest position and remove the bumper pads, if you have them. Also, remove any large toys that an active toddler may stand on to escape from the crib.

Your baby's crib needs only a firm, tight-fitting mattress and crib sheet. If you can fit more than two fingers between the edge of the mattress and crib side, the mattress is too small. An infant can suffocate if his/her head or body becomes wedged between the mattress and the crib sides. Blankets, stuffed animals, and pillows are all suffocation risks for children under age one. Crib bumpers also fall into the same category.

Once your baby can push up on his/her knees, remove any crib mobiles and other such decorations. When your baby can stand in his crib and the railing top is chest height for him or her — and the mattress is at its lowest point — then it's time to move them out of the crib.

Changing Table

The optimum changing table is one with straps to secure that wiggling baby. Falls are most likely to happen when diapers or outfits are being changed. However, even with straps, you should keep one hand on the baby at all times. Baby changing essentials, such as lotion, hand gel, and other supplies, should be stored in a nearby drawer or shelf beyond the baby's reach.

Toy Box

The Home Safety Council recommends storing toys in bins or boxes without lids. If your toy chest does have a lid, it should also have a spring-loaded mechanical arm that prevents the lid from falling on your baby's hand or trapping him if he manages to climb inside. If it doesn't have such a device, you can retrofit your toy box or chest with a kit from the hardware store.

Gates

The gate at the top of your stairs should screw into the wall or doorjamb because pressure-mounted gates may not stand up to a determined toddler. The U.S. Consumer Product Safety Commission (CPSC) warns against accordion-style gates with V-shaped or diamond-shaped openings (the kind we grew up with); they can strangle kids.

You only need six items: a crib (somewhere to sleep), a changing table (somewhere to clean and dress), a nursery hamper (for used baby outfits), a nightstand and lamp (for feeding supplies), a diaper hamper, and a rocker where you will feed your baby. After that, the rest is up to you! Some of the questions I am often asked are: Where should I place the furniture? How do I design the room? Below I have listed some helpful tips to get you started.

- PLACING THE CRIB: The crib should be placed first, in an area that will keep the baby out of drafts or direct sunlight and consider the baby's view of any of murals or interesting features in the room. Try to place the crib close to the entrance of the room. There are many crib options, including corner cribs and mini cribs.
- PLACING THE ROCKER: The rocker should be close to the nightstand and window. It is relaxing to be able to look out the window when feeding the baby. Also make sure you can see the clock from the rocker. Rockers should be placed on rugs.
- PLACING THE CHANGING TABLE: The changing table should be close to the crib, and the nursery hamper should be close to the changing table. There are dresser/ changing table options that get two jobs done with one piece of furniture. Corner changing tables can be used to take advantage of that empty corner space.

One item I would add if you have the budget is shelves. Shelves use no floor space and they can be positioned around the nursery to provide convenient storage spots. However, do not put shelves near the crib. To check out some cute shelves, go to the website www.csnbaby.com.

Now for the fun part. After you select the colors, fabrics, and finishes to create your dream-come-true nursery, how do you start? Where do you find those darling fabrics you see in magazines?

In designing a nursery, I ask my clients to provide me with a selection of ideas that they like for the room. Clients may find these photos on the Internet or in books and magazines. This will help you to determine your design style and the color combinations you might like. Once you choose a style, it will affect every element in the room. There are a plethora of styles out there or you can create your own.

When I design a room, I start with the floor plan and furniture. The first thing to do is measure the rooms; make sure to note where the doors and windows are. From these dimensions, you can develop your base plan. The next task is to select the furniture and know its dimensions. I recommend drawing the furniture to scale, cutting it out, and placing it on the plan.

Here are a few things to keep in mind while executing this task:

- Establish a focal point for the nursery. It could be a window, crib, or a mural.
- Maintain balance by placing the furniture around the room evenly. Spread out colors and patterns and maintain a balance between wood and upholstery. Use draperies, linens, and pillows to add a punch of color.
- Make sure the scale of the furniture is proportionate to the size of the room.
- Try out different arrangements of furniture. By placing the furniture on an angle, a small room can appear bigger.

After the plan is set and furniture selected, I begin the process of selecting fabrics and finishes and designing the drapery treatments. I start this process by selecting a key fabric (the one with the pattern on it). Some of my favorite sources for lead fabrics are Christian Fischbacher (www.fischbacher.ch/pages/en/interior_fabrics) and Designers Guild (www.designersguild.com) for modern fabrics and Jane Churchill (www.janechurchill.com) for traditional fabrics. I generally use these fabrics in the drapery treatments or wallpaper. From there, I can choose colors for upholstery and bedding.

Courtesy of Designers Guild (www.designersguild.com).

Recognized by her peers for design excellence, Jo Ann Alston brings thirty years of experience and consummate skills to create interior designs of exceptional beauty, comfort, and grace. Her ability to meld European and Asian influences into stunning traditional and contemporary interiors is reflective of her extensive travels and study of cultures abroad. Clients marvel at the in-depth manner in which she assesses their needs and her total commitment to achieving that vision. They also appreciate her unique talent for resolving unanticipated issues with brilliant solutions that please all. Architects, builders, and contractors rely on her professional expertise in planning and designing spaces, lighting, windows, doors, and other structural elements. Her close attention to detail also ensures everything is implemented to exact specification.

Ms. Alston is an ASID award-winning certified interior designer. She is the recipient of two Design Excellence awards from the New Jersey ASID chapter and her work is regularly featured in local magazines. It was also featured in *Today's Historic Interiors* (published by Schiffer Publishing and written by E. Ashley Rooney), and this year her work was featured on an episode of NBC's *House Smarts*.

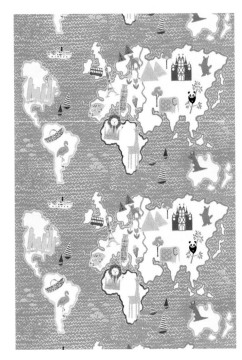

Courtesy of Designers Guild (www.designersguild.com).

Designers such as Sissy + Marley and the others in this book know how to appeal to children. *Courtesy of Marco Ricca Photography.*

DESIGN TIP: *Prepare your nursery the way a bird prepares her nest. Lovingly select each piece and take care in placing them just right. Make it cozy enough that they want to stay for a while, but be prepared for the day they find their wings.*

THE GENDER NEUTRAL NURSERY

Lilli's Design Presentation Board for Black, White, and Bold Hollywood Regency for Baby. *Courtesy of Lilli Design.*

What a wondrous world this little one will grow to know and love. This gender-neutral nursery designed by dBk Interiors was inspired by the crib and changing table from Corsican Furniture Co. The lavender of a sunset and the greens of the grasses make us think of the plains of Africa. The woven grass blind has a room-darkening shade behind and a flat scalloped valance above. The majestic giraffe lamp is from Lamps Plus. The antique rocker and chest of drawers are reminiscent of the British colonials who traveled to exotic places with all of their homeland possessions.

dBk replaced the flat closet doors with more louvered bi-fold doors, adding texture and architectural interest. The hardware was changed to antique brass animals similar to the crib and changing table. The grass green wall-to-wall carpet is soft and cushy as opposed to the other hard surfaces used. All the fabrics and bedding are from Serena and Lily. The soft plush ducky rocker and stuffed elephant remind us that this explorer has a lot of growing yet to do. This nursery was featured in *201 Home Magazine. Courtesy of Stephen Michael Garey Photography.*

17

Modern Yellow and Aqua Nursery

Lilli Design used soft taupe gray from Farrow & Ball's designer palette to create a serene and fresh feel for this modern gender-neutral nursery. Bold shades of yellow and aqua offset white clean-lined furnishings. The bold yellow and white chevron pattern on the ottoman is not only a perfect spot to rest tired feet, but also adds an intense pop of color to the neutral gray flooring.

Graphic trellis patterns give the room a modern yet transitional feel and are featured on the dresser lamp, crib bed skirt, and the shaded linen pendant. The crib bedding brings in the gray, yellow, and aqua palette in a variety of interesting patterns.

Floor-to-ceiling built-in bookshelves offer many places to display favorite books and photos as well as unique objects from baby's growing collection of toys.

Just off the bedroom, this bathroom was tiled in bright white with a white Carrera marble vanity top and coordinating gray walls to tie in with the nursery. Pops of yellow in the accessories and linens bring in the colors from the nursery to create a harmonized space.

A Nursery for Curious George

Shirley Fadden of Wallflowers often uses trees in designing a nursery. She points out that the baby can grow into them and enjoy the room for many years. Trees are also unisex. Snails, mushrooms, ferns, butterflies, birds, and flowers add color and interest.

Yellow Nursery

Joani Stewart-Georgi of Montana Avenue Interiors created a charming yellow nursery for a mother-to-be who didn't know the sex of the baby. The crib, changing table, rocker for two, and the window and bed coverings are by Bambini. The closet is by Closets by Design and the carpeting by Contempo. Nursery rhyme paintings adorn the wall. *Photo by Douglas Hill.*

Eco-Chic Nursery

Designed by Susan Fredman, Ruth Delf, and Kathy Hoffman of Susan Fredman Design Group, this nursery was a part of Healthy Home 2010: Designer Showcase and Tour, which raised the bar on sustainable design by focusing on healthy indoor air quality. All items in the room, including the furniture, bedding, wall coverings, rugs, toys, etc. are non-toxic and contain low or no volatile organic compounds (VOCs) and thus contribute to healthy indoor air quality. The furniture is from Q Collection Junior, which is GreenGuard certified and uses 100 percent FSC certified woods. The rug, by Orly Shabahang, is made from all-natural materials and colored with vegetable dye, and the wall covering is by American Clay, a natural earth plaster colored with all-natural dyes. *Courtesy of Nick Novelli of Novelli PhotoDesign.*

The giraffe mural was the inspiration for this room created by Jen Meyer Interiors. The pop of orange gets picked up with West Elm's simple drum table necessary for books/bottles and midnight feedings. The light fixture is an inexpensive find from IKEA. *Courtesy of Jeremy Swanson*.

Originally, an animal print was going to be used for the drapes, but Jen found this wonderful forest print. The deer with the squirrels and rabbits happily meander through the forest. The eighteen-inch orange border adds some fun, keeps it light, and connects the drape to the giraffe mural. The inverted pleat at the top gives a fuller drape and more casual pleating of the fabric. Drape is lined with black out lining for restful naps and nights. *Courtesy of Jeremy Swanson.*

Most of the home is furnished with a lot of mid-century furnishings. Luckily, nursery furniture now has some wonderful modern options. The crib and changing table are from Oeuf NYC – the Sparrow Collection. The organic cotton flannel blanket is from ABC Home. *Courtesy of Jeremy Swanson*.

The mother-to-be wanted a gender neutral space for her new daughter. The home is situated in Colorado with views of surrounding mountains from its windows. Built in 1981, the home was an experiment in green living prior to the current trend. Walls and floors are bare concrete to absorb the powerful sun, which flows through oversized windows to hold the warmth throughout the winter days. *Courtesy of Jeremy Swanson*.

THE GIRL'S NURSERY

Lilli's Design Presentation Board for Classic Elegant Nursery in Shades of White. *Courtesy of Lilli Design.*

Elegant Heirloom Haven

Says Megan Clark of CasaPosh, for whose daughter this room was created: "This timeless space is my most treasured project as a designer because it was created with the utmost love and care for my own beautiful baby girl. I knew I wanted a space that could grow with her throughout the years and withstand the different phases of her childhood — a space that was elegant and composed, yet whimsical enough to host even the most well imagined tea party guests. I wanted to fill it with beautiful heirlooms that reminded her of the generations of family that anxiously awaited her arrival." *Courtesy of Jim Landers.*

"Using a neutral mix of painted finishes, warm wood grains, silks, burlap, and a delicate crystal chandelier, I created a space that exudes rustic charm. The soft gray, oatmeal, and ivory palette teases the senses with just enough color to add interest, but also allows the furniture in the room to tell the story…the story of Helen." *Courtesy of Jim Landers*.

Vintage Chic Nursery

Chocolate brown walls and painted ivory wainscoting create a timeless backdrop to the bold and unexpected colors featured in the bedding and accessories. Katie Reynolds created a vintage feel with the use of an updated damask pattern on the custom robin's egg blue and fuchsia crib bedding. Neutrals on the chair and flooring ground the overall palette and allow the bright color in the bedding and silk drapery to be the stars of the room.

A fun vintage find, the scalloped silver mirror was salvaged from an estate sale and becomes a delicate centerpiece over the hand-distressed dresser. Modern artwork in shades of pink and aqua works in tandem with the overall composition to give the room a transitional, eclectic feel. A beautiful smocked silk dress fit for a princess is hanging from a customized crystal dresser knob.

Victoriana Pink

What a lovely, serene space for this baby girl to reside in! This nursery, designed by dBk Interiors, was inspired by the lovely pink and white toile bedding by Angel Baby. In order not to become cloyingly sweet, dBk countered it with a fresh lime green. The stripe lining valance and bed skirt match the green walls and seersucker plaid on the Four Seasons rocking chair.

A lovely coronet holds a white sheer and pale pink Swiss dot from Kravet Fabrics, adding height to the overall design. A charming pair of white iron silhouette wall sconces of children at play flank the crib and adds to the Victorian charm. A bronze scalloped and antiqued mirror table from Pierre Deux provides a handy space for story time books. A low antiqued dresser is decorated with a bronze fretwork and bees, sweet as honey. dBk chose wall-to-wall carpet in a neutral wheat lattice pattern for its durability and cleanability. *Courtesy of Stephen Michael Garey Photography.*

This Lilli Design nursery was all about glitz and glam. Starting with a rich palette of decadent purple and green from the client, the room has a decidedly elegant tone without losing sight of the baby. Bold eggplant silk draperies matching the wall color perfectly flank the south facing window. Touches of sparkle were added with a mirrored accent table and delicate crystal dressed sconces on either side of the changing station.

The crib features custom made silk and velvet bedding fit for a princess in rich jewel tones. A damask pattern was hand-stenciled over the crib, and custom painted framed artwork completes the look. A plush damask rug in chocolate and olive green adds interest and dimension to the floor.

Reminiscent of a Victorian frame, a carved white mirror hangs at the room's entry, and a whimsical growth chart winds up on an adjacent wall. The bedding would not be complete without a custom mobile over the crib to entertain and soothe baby.

The sophisticated black molding is the perfect contrast to the pink and white walls. The zebra rug and matching lamps add an element of fun, and the white furniture ties it all in. *Courtesy of Vanessa deLeon Associates.*

This nursery is perfect for a sophisticated little princess with style. Designer Vanessa deLeon paired a pastel pink, black, and white color scheme for an elegant boutique feel. She then added this black vinyl chandelier decal, which adds elegance and a modern element of depth and texture. *Courtesy of Vanessa deLeon Associates.*

Shirley Fadden of Wallflowers used a dark and woody looking monogram to pull in the color of the dresser and balance the crib in the opposite corner. The heart carved into the tree and the butterflies are in remembrance of a family member. The red and dark green accents in the mushrooms and décor move the color around the room for balance and create pops of color.

Sugar and Spice Paradise

Lilli Design created a room fit for a princess with a sugary sweet palette of bright pink and white accented with touches of yellow and green. The oversized chair is perfect for snuggling and late-night feedings. A silk-like rug with a bold and colorful graphic floral print sets the palette for the entire room and gives the room a true wow factor.

A scalloped mirror adds a vintage touch over the distressed white dresser. A hand-painted growth chart hangs delicately from a ribbon and adds a personalized touch to the room. The distressed white crib features custom hand-made bedding in graphic-patterned cotton.

To create a dramatic backdrop for the space, a delicate ribbon stencil is featured on the crib wall. The pink ribbons add depth and drama, and then for added drama, modern gallery framed newborn photography was layered on top.

THE BOY'S NURSERY

Lilli's Design Presentation Board for an Urban Safari Nursery. *Courtesy of Lilli Design.*

This nursery design by Joani Stewart-Georgi of Montana Avenue Interiors began with a nautical design centered on the lighthouse. The father was so glad to have a son after his two daughters that he became involved in the room's decor. The red leather fold-out/convertible sofa designed by Cantoni opens to a twin bed for the mother or nanny. *Photo by Douglas Hill.*

When the baby begins exploring, he can enjoy the wonders of the ocean designed by Sedi Pak Studios. *Photo by Douglas Hill.*

The carpeting and window and floor pillow covering fabrication are by Contempo Floor Coverings. The window covering and floor pillow fabric is by Ralph Lauren. The lighthouse lamp and sailboat knobs are by Rosenberry Rooms. *Photo by Douglas Hill.*

Even the knobs on the changing table's drawer are hand-painted with sailboats. *Photo by Douglas Hill.*

This design coordinates beautifully with the Sailing Away bedding from Gordonsbury Company. *Photo by Douglas Hill.*

43

Sissy + Marley's goal was to create a room that was organic, soothing, stylish, and modern in a warm way. Using Baby Elephant Walk wallpaper by Jill Malek (elephants are a sign of good luck!), they covered the walls and closet doors to give the room a warm and polished look. The knitted pendant light, custom made and hand embroidered artwork, super closet, and modern but warm furniture make this room stand out. *Courtesy of Marco Ricca Photography.*

The barnstormer biplane model inspires this nursery created by dBk. Done in All-American shades of red, white, and blue, stars and stripes forever, it welcomes a darling baby boy.

The airplane models are from Authentic Models Inc. The crib from Benecia Foundry is in an antique brass finish, as is the hardware and changing table (not pictured). The bench and dresser are custom pieces from Ron Fisher in a crackle barn red over buttermilk finish with specialty knobs in a fun blue and white star shape. The bedding, window, and chair fabric is from Serena and Lily. An area rug, from Sturbridge Yankee Workshop, anchors the room's center and adds a spark of interest to the broadloom carpet. Sturdy wooden blinds control the lighting and privacy issues in the room, but the coach shade valance with adjustable suspenders adds a whimsical softness to the window. One can picture our flyboy revving up his biplane's engine and surveying his Americana landscape dressed in overalls and suspenders. *201 Home Magazine* featured this nursery. *Courtesy of Stephen Michael Garey Photography.*

Yippee ki yay! Shirley Fadden, principal of Wallflowers, created a western-themed nursery for young Ethan.

Initially, his closet was painted like a bandana.

Later, she turned it into a red built-in closet. Boys don't need a full-length closet, she points out. The dresser is built into the closet to conserve floor space.

The shelves were built into the dormers as a space saver. Cubbies built into the walls are used to store desk items.

There was no room for a desk, so that was built in as well.

From Baby to Teen

Designed by Kingsley Belcher Knauss of KBK Interior Design, this nursery expresses the client's desire to provide a crisp space spare of clutter. A block-style animal print with contrasting blue and white gingham was chosen for the tailored valances and custom crib bumpers. Fabrics were chosen to coordinate with ready-made bedding and other "off the shelf" decor.

The three-year-old boy received his dream of a "race car bed" and added his own design elements in the form of "sticker art" and posters. KBK was called back onto the scene to rescue this design.

By the time the child was five, the client decided that storage in this small room was needed. The child's fantasy of a metallic "golden" bedroom with blue and orange was fulfilled by placing metallic wallcovering behind the custom headboard wallwashed by down lights. Knowing that the gold may be short-lived, this wall covering was used sparingly, and the other walls were painted a warm caramel color. Built-ins provide toy and book storage on either side of a removable twin bed, and floor space was gained for playing. If this room is ever converted to a guest room, a queen bed may be placed between the built-ins. Toy storage was added below the bed, but this could have easily been a trundle bed, if desired.

A pullout tray works in place of nightstands, and adjustable reading lights were added for storytime. Storage compartments have dividers to make for easier organization of toys or future clothing. Grommets were added in the countertop for electrical access for plugging in a clock and electronic games.

Down the Bunny Trail

A pom-pom trim travels down the side of the plaid shower curtain in this nursery suite. The curtain is hung on a wooden rod enhanced with a bunny tieback and finial. Nickel bunny hardware has been added to the bathroom cabinet doors in keeping with the Peter Rabbit themed bedroom. *Courtesy of Marisa Pellegrini.*

This nursery was originally designed for the clients' two older girls, but the third time they had a son! Patricia Montalbano of the Montalbano Design Group had designed this room with a neutral gender Peter Rabbit motif. After choosing a new paint color for the new little boy's room, the design firm had their workroom redesign the window treatments as well as the custom shades by removing and replacing the trim for a more masculine feel. The existing chandelier was replaced with lighting designed to resemble a hot air balloon lamp and a new lampshade was custom designed for the table lamp. The custom-made patchwork area rug is more in keeping with a little boy and can "grow up" along with him. All the client's former furniture fit perfectly in the new décor, which goes to prove that redesigning a nursery need not be a costly venture. *Courtesy of Marisa Pellegrini.*

A Soothing Lullaby

The blue backdrop chosen for this little boy's nursery by Marguerite Rodgers creates a calming palette. A vintage bent wood rocker, Shaker ottoman, and antique rug add traditional comforts. Built-in bookcases provide room for storage and the display of books and toys. Open space offers an area to play. Traditional elements with non-traditional applications, such as the fireplace filled with logs, add to the room's eclectic feel while keeping the child safe from harm. A framed map above the fireplace hints at an adventurous life ahead and is the final touch on this out-of-this-world nursery. *Courtesy of ©Halkin Photography LLC.*

A fashion designer, the mother-to-be had her own ideas about what she wanted her baby's room to look like when she contracted with Joani Stewart-Georgi of Montana Avenue Interiors. The dark chocolate finish on the crib makes it resemble adult furniture. The first thing you see upon entering the room is the baby's name in large-scale letters. The colorful rug and the skirt on the bed give color and whimsy to the room. Used with permission from *Better Homes & Gardens*© magazine. ©2004 Meredith Corporation. All Rights reserved.

A bright Angela Adams rug covers the floor with its colorful design swirling around. Children's blocks lie on the rug. Used with permission from *Better Homes & Gardens*© magazine. ©2004 Meredith Corporation. All Rights reserved.

Montana Avenue Interiors designed the bathroom specifically with a baby in mind. The sink was placed in the corner so there is plenty of counter space for a baby tub. The firm also designed a step system that hides under the cabinet to be used when the baby needs to reach the sink. The tiles are small green glass squares that cover the wall as well as the counter. A chocolate-framed mirror that matches the cabinetry is set into a Carrera marble frame with the sconces installed against it. The cabinet pulls were also green glass with a design to go with the rest of the tile. A storage cabinet holds all of the required elements for a baby's bath, with shelves on the side allowing for easy access to those important items that a mom needs to reach with one hand while holding the baby with the other. Used with permission from *Better Homes & Gardens*© magazine. ©2004 Meredith Corporation. All Rights reserved.

This unit holds many of those infant necessities.

Transportation Room

Everyone knows that small boys like trucks, planes, and boats for a long time — sometimes even into adulthood. Shirley Fadden, principal of Wallflowers, designed a room focusing on cars, trucks, and planes for one young client.

Shirley's design is throughout the room: on the clock, the book ends, even the pillows. *Courtesy of Lilli Design.*

When designing a room for Sebastian, Sissy + Marley believed it was important to create a space he would grow into. "We wanted his room to be sophisticated, chic, playful, and functional. We always dreamed of having double doors that led into the nursery, so we added them." *Courtesy of Marco Ricca Photography.*

"We wanted Sebastian's room to be filled with art and pieces that would spark his imagination. We had images from the book *Creature* by Andrew Zuckerman framed in white modern frames. A stuffed deer head by Tamar Mogendorff sits above the closet doors. The map of the world hangs behind his bed so he can dream of all the places he will travel to one day." *Courtesy of Marco Ricca Photography.*

The room is shades of white, cream, and washed out blue. The furniture is clean and modern using washed natural oak and white lacquer. Cabine crib and dresser are from the Netto collection. *Courtesy of Marco Ricca Photography.*

"Sebastian loves this pretty deer (by Tamar Mogendorff) that watches over him with lashes so long, a heart shaped nose, and the most fabulous camouflage antlers." *Courtesy of Marco Ricca Photography.*

The firm created a wall of framed images. The leather mirrors by Serena & Lily bring a masculine feel to the room: rich, classic, and well traveled. The Alto Rocker in white leather is a perfect spot for mother and child. *Courtesy of Marco Ricca Photography.*

Susan Huckvale Arann of American & International Designs, Inc. created visual interest by incorporating blocks of color from the Ralph Lauren collection in the corner of the ceiling molding. The Pacific Rim bookcase and the Bernhardt headboard in a red mahogany finish showcase the Ralph Lauren nautical bedding. The custom cornice from Island Upholstery repeats the bedding fabric inside a red framework to add interest without overwhelming the room. The hardwood floor shows off the nautical rug that Susan found on a seaside trip. The lighting from Richmond Chandelier illuminates the faux tray ceiling. The nautical feel is complemented by the introduction of the silver accents on the bookcase and lighting fixture, which have coordinating chrome finishes.

Lilli's Design Presentation Board for Luxe Green Nursery. *Courtesy of Lilli Design.*

There is a place for each baby in this ethereal space of calming colors. Stephanie of Marsh and Clark designed a setting where three cribs float on a fluffy cloud. *Courtesy of Elisabeth Fall Photography.*

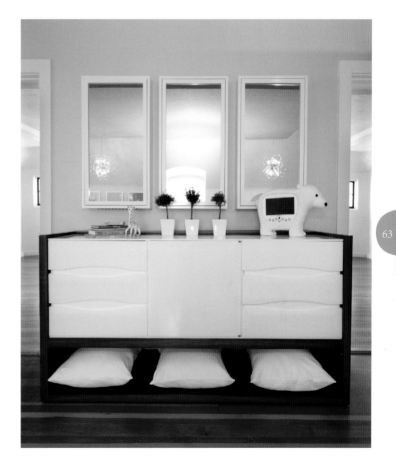

The welcoming Stingray rocking chair — nestled in a corner — has room enough for three. *Courtesy of Elisabeth Fall Photography.*

Three's a crowd, so space-saving is crucial. This custom-made credenza is crowned with mirrors that fold-down, becoming a changing table. *Courtesy of Elisabeth Fall Photography.*

Lit from within, the perforated constellation design on the front of each bench panel turns these ingenious perches adorning each crib into seriously sophisticated night-lights. *Courtesy of Elisabeth Fall Photography*.

Hand-cut Mya Romanoff wallpaper accentuates the light's twinkling glow alongside the cozy nook of a built-in window seat. *Courtesy of Elisabeth Fall Photography.*

The mesmerizing sparkle of this modern light fixture is designed to keep each baby entertained. It doubles as a very safe mobile. *Courtesy of Elisabeth Fall Photography.*

The main crib structure, built from Medite, a sustainable formaldehyde-free, FSC-certified recycled fiberboard, evokes sophisticated, modern architectural forms. Zero-VOC water-based white lacquer elevates the design with a brilliant sheen. *Courtesy of Elisabeth Fall Photography.*

Twin Infants' Green Room

This nursery started with very high-end geometric carpeting from Patterson, Flynn & Martin. The client was so in love with the carpet that when she found a new home, she took it with her. Her twin boys currently have their nursery carpeting as a rug in their new bedroom. Evelyn Benatar of New York Interior Design pulled the color scheme, which is shades of green and brown, directly from the carpeting. Striped wall covering, found at Wolf Gordon, was placed on the far wall as a feature wall, incorporating all of the desired colors. The cream fabric with green fish was purchased at Donghia to create the custom-made valance. Matching white cribs were selected from Oeuf, with a dresser from Nursery Works to complement them. The wide rocker also came from Nursery Works and was upholstered in a fern green mohair fabric from Donghia. This nursery was designed to be young and fun. *Courtesy of Tony Cacarco Photography.*

THE TODDLER'S BEDROOM

"The potential possibilities of any child are the most intriguing and stimulating in all creation."

– Ray L. Wilbur,
3rd president of
Stanford University

GIRL'S BEDROOM

Lilli Design's Presentation Board for East Meets West Global Bazaar. *Courtesy of Lilli Design.*

Mod Flower Power Girl's Room

Evelyn Benatar of New York Interior Design got her inspiration from the red and orange flower-power Marimekko wall covering from Donghia. Her goal was to create a very cool, funky little girl's room for an Upper East Side Manhattan apartment. The bed was custom-made and upholstered in white patent leather. Instead of choosing modern furniture, she chose a black distressed Louis XVI style dresser and nightstand from Grange, giving the room an eclectic feeling. At Stark Carpet, she purchased a silver shag carpet chosen for comfort. The ultimate goal was to make this room reminiscent of the 1970s, but with a fresh twist. With that in mind, Evelyn purchased a funky table lamp from Design Within Reach and a playful light fixture from MSK Lighting. The small chair was essential because it is low to the ground and comfortable. The window treatments were custom-made with fabric from Donghia, and the black wood toggle trim was purchased at Samuel & Sons. *Courtesy of Tony Cacarco Photography.*

The custom-made bookshelf and built-in desk were designed with a small child in mind. The backing of the bookshelf was painted light pink and was originally designed with the intention of filling the space with cool, fun accessories that could represent the child. This was important because the accessories could also grow and change. The bookshelf accessories were mostly purchased at ABC Carpet and West Elm, giving the room its finishing touches. This room can take this child from age 2-1/2 all the way through her "tween" years. *Courtesy of Tony Cacarco Photography.*

Patricia Montalbano of the Montalbano Design Group created a charming bedroom for a five-year-old girl named "Jenny" in a lovely Victorian home. The family's love of antiques is reflected in this room as well as the rest of the house. Patricia chose a collection of antique dolls to accessorize the room. A charming place to play, the window seat also acts as a display space for the collection. © *image/dennis krukowski, all rights reserved.*

The Group designed a twin size bed to look like a large chaise lounge. With its upholstered arms and back, it is a comfortable area to curl up in. The architectural proportions of the room called for an illusion of a canopy over the bed and bringing down some of the ceiling height. Jenny loved to read so the Group added two slip-covered chairs with special detailing in the coordinating fabric. All fabric, wall covering, and trims were carefully selected to enhance this room and to take Jenny into adolescence. © *image/dennis krukowski, all rights reserved.*

Importance of Ceilings

Sarah Elizabeth Clinger of Lifestyle Interior Design points out that while ceilings are typically ignored, they can play a significant role in the appearance of a child's room and how the child feels about that space when he is in the room.

Ceilings offer psychological meaning: they are the roofs over our heads. The ceiling provides security, it defines spatial relationships in the room, and in the end it offers protection. Aesthetically, ceilings add interest to a boxy space. They can lower or raise the feeling of a ceiling in the room. A low ceiling should be lighter and brighter than the walls. Extra high ceilings should have intense color coatings, like the color of the sky or any high contrast that appeals to the wall color.

If the room has a vaulted ceiling, then you have interesting architecture. The ceiling will be the first thing your eye goes to as you enter the room. Play up the architecture with contrasting color or a thematic border that enhances the amusement aspect of a room. The border will attract the eye to the edge as opposed to the center, making the room appear larger than it is.

Sarah Elizabeth Clinger added texture and interest to a boxy room when she added this plaid ceiling treatment and a border of running horses.

Reading Corner

Susan Huckvale Arann of American & International Designs, Inc. designed a wonderful reading corner for a three-year-old to curl up with a good book and a jelly sandwich. She used a durable, washable slip-covered barrel chair from IKEA, an initialed pillow from Pottery Barn, which gives our little sweetheart a sense of ownership in the space, and a custom ottoman covered with three different fabrics that relate to the bedding. The area rug is from Pottery Barn, with a wall covering from Seabrook in toile depicting colonial children in playful scenes.

Making a "pretty" room for this two-year-old girl was the goal for Hilary Unger of Perianth Interior Design. Pinks, greens, and yellows were the colors used to create a breathtaking princess room in White Plains, New York. The child's chair is from John Roselli. *Photo by Michael Falco.*

Built-in cabinetry was designed to create a focal point for the room. The bed, which doubles as a day bed, is decorated with an array of back and throw pillows and sits in front of a floral fabric wall. The fabric was paper-backed and treated so that it could be used as "wallpaper." *Photo by Michael Falco.*

It's all in the details, as purple throw pillows from Gracious Home bring out the best of the colors in the floral focal fabric from Pierre Frey. *Photo by Michael Falco.*

The built-in cabinetry was painted white like the rest of the trim in the room, and soft yellow-striped wallpaper was installed below the new chair rail around the room. Green carpet, a bright pink bed skirt, a beautiful chandelier, and lots of color creates a wonderful fairy-tale feeling for the bedroom. *Photo by Michael Falco.*

The built-in cabinetry followed the angled lines of the ceiling and is decorated with books and knickknacks special to the little girl who lives in this room. Silk checkered fabric and tassels from Samuel and Sons soften the window and create the quintessential girls' valance. *Photo by Michael Falco.*

Suite Caroline

Patricia Montalbano of the Montalbano Design Group created this "grown-up" five-year-old girl's bedroom suite. Her custom-made French iron bed with canopy in a lovely iris base with a floral and bluebird motif sets the stage. The custom-made French bookcase coordinates with the bed by featuring a striped iris and pansy interior and a floral and butterfly motif on the exterior. The custom-made beaded table lamps with amethyst flowers harmonize with the antique silver finished crystal and amethyst beaded chandelier. As the big sister, she must have her own personalized Queen Anne side chair with her own monogram. Floral end panels with ribbon ruche trim overlay lace panels at the window. The oval multi-colored braided rug brings the whole color palette together. The design of this room was meant to follow her well into her teen years. *Courtesy of Marisa Pellegrini.*

This bedroom designed by Susan Fredman, Ruth Delf, and Kathy Hoffman of Susan Fredman Design Group was a part of Healthy Home 2010: Designer Showcase and Tour, which raised the bar on sustainable design by focusing on healthy indoor air quality. All of the items in the room, including the furniture, bedding, wall coverings, and rugs are non-toxic and contain low or no volatile organic compounds (VOCs) and thus contribute to healthy indoor air quality. The bed is made in the USA and contains no VOCs or urea-formaldehyde; the nightstands and chairs are reclaimed antiques updated with no-VOC paints or stains; the rug, by Orly Shabahang, is made from all-natural materials and colored with vegetable dye; the bedding is all organic; the paint is from the Benjamin Moore Natura line and contains no VOCs; and the mural behind the bed is painted on a piece of canvas that can be removed as the child grows older and can be used by another person. The furniture was designed to grow with the girl so that it doesn't need to be replaced as she ages, and the room can be easily updated with new accessories and non-toxic paints and finishes. *Courtesy of Nick Novelli of Novelli PhotoDesign.*

This girl's room is a nod to the family's heritage. Designed by Marguerite Rodgers, the room incorporates early American furniture with punches of pink and yellow. Grown-up details, like the adjustable table lamps, add sophistication without detracting from the youthful feel of the room. A traditional bathroom with modern amenities features a large tub perfect for bubble baths. A mix of antique pieces, feminine fabrics, wood plank walls, and patchwork quilt tile mosaic create a playfully inviting space. The past meets the present in these rooms that step into a storybook and transport you back in time. *Courtesy of ©Halkin Photography LLC.*

79

Sissy+Marley's goal was to transform Ava's nursery into a big kid room that would grow with her. Working with five-year-old Ava, they created the ultimate room filled with pieces fit for a little girl who loves, loves, loves pink. They chose chic furniture that will get her well past preschool and linens that were girly and classic. Fit for a princess, the Cabana Collection canopy bed, bolster pillows, dresser, and desk are from Duc Duc, New York City. Sissy+Marley wanted to fulfill their young client's request for a pink room, but execute it in a very chic way that she would still love years from now! *Courtesy of Marco Ricca Photography.*

Any girl (big or little) would enjoy primping in front of these Horchow Venetian mirrors. *Courtesy of Marco Ricca Photography.*

A candy pink pouf adds punches of Ava's must-have color. Soft Moroccan poufs in kids' rooms make great little spots to perch on. The Moroccan inspired rug and pouf add a bit of bohemian chic to the room. *Courtesy of Marco Ricca Photography.*

These Namhee fabric-wrapped bird hooks are the perfect spot for her jewels. *Courtesy of Marco Ricca Photography.*

This is the prettiest squirrel we have ever seen sitting on a bureau. It is handmade by Tamar Mogendorff. *Courtesy of Marco Ricca Photography.*

Whimsical handmade pieces like fabric-covered bird hooks and a linen inspiration board were hung to display Ava's necklaces and her artwork. *Courtesy of Marco Ricca Photography.*

These framed Hermes scarf prints from the book *The Hermes Scarf History & Mystique* by Nadine Coleno are beautiful. *Courtesy of Marco Ricca Photography.*

This writing desk is perfect for project time and homework. *Courtesy of Marco Ricca Photography.*

Sandra Clinger of Lifestyle Interior Design trimmed the pencil point canopy and window valance in contrasting tape. They reinforce each other and calm the space through continuity. She covered the rocker with hand-painted canvas to keep the room playful. It balances the lively plaid pencil point bed skirt too. She installed a light over the bed and under the canopy to secretly allow relaxed reading before sleep. What a "lift" for this little one to climb into her bed! She climbs on three fully upholstered, cheery steps. The duvet cover is a production item, available in discount stores, washing machine ready to deal with stains and spills. The walls and ceiling were painted a whiter shade of pink to animate this bedroom.

Phyllis Harbinger of Design Concepts/Interiors says, "We took our cue from the bedding — the pink and black polka dots were very playful. I also loved the bold contrast of the black and white cotton stripe. We designed a headboard that played with the scale of the room, bringing your eye up to the large hot pink-painted beam, which reinforced the color scheme. We designed the window awning treatments using a replay of the bedding fabrics. We added a tassel trim at the bottom of the blackout roller shade to make them more interesting and feminine. This client is clearly not afraid of color!" *Courtesy of Ken Gabrielson Photography.*

Joani Stewart-Georgi of Montana Avenue Interiors designed this room for sisters, aged two and four, whose mom was expecting again. They needed a fantastic room so they wouldn't be jealous of the new baby. The firm and client decided pink and brown was sophisticated and cute, yet still retaining a little princess look. The round cushions at the end of the beds are really lounging pillows for the girls when they lie about on the floor. *Photo by Douglas Hill.*

Montana Avenue Interiors custom-designed the bedding and headboards using Contempo Floor Coverings. The painting above is a ribbon with the names of both girls. *Photo by Douglas Hill.*

The Thea Segal Designs play table was custom painted with the same pattern as the fabric on the window cornices. *Photo by Douglas Hill*.

The window treatments were also custom and added whimsy to the room. The firm found the hanging butterflies in the corner to add that fun note. The Stanley Furniture wardrobes are small enough for the girls to get to their own clothes and feel grown-up. Montana Avenue Interiors also built-in a bookcase to encourage reading and keeping things in their place. *Photo by Douglas Hill*.

84

Susan Fredman, Barbara Ince, and Gina Valenti of Susan Fredman Design Group designed this room for a young girl who has an interest in theater and loves to dream. The designers built a stage area inside of the window bay with drapery that can be closed during rehearsals and to introduce performances (a separate set of window treatments can be used for privacy from the outside). Light blue ottomans in the stage area provide a pop of color and can be used as props and additional seating for performances. The designers continued the drapery theme above the bed with a custom design, opting to forgo a traditional canopy. The queen-sized bed was positioned with the long side against the wall to create more of a stage-like feel. The color palette, inspired by the girl's love of pink, teal, and monkeys, culminates in the custom bedding. *Courtesy of Nick Novelli of Novelli PhotoDesign*.

Pink Plaid and Toile

Designed by Kingsley Belcher Knauss, ASID KBK Interior Design, this little girl's room features beautifully carved furniture with upholstered elements. The footboard and fabric panel in the armoire provide custom detail highlighting the ivory and pink toile. An appliqué pillow with a child's initial and a toile bunny fabricated from one of the room's fabrics are an affordable way to add a special touch to any child's room. *Courtesy of Paul S. Bartholomew Photography, Inc.*

Sophisticated Girl's Room

This room created by Evelyn Benatar of New York Interior Design began with the purchase of an incredible, colorful rug from ABC Home. The rug gave the firm the color scheme, which consisted of pinks, yellows, and oranges. The twin beds were custom-made, and the bedding from ABC Home was added to give a fresh, clean look. For extra lighting, the firm purchased sconces and track lighting from Lee's Lighting. Two sconces were placed near the bedside, one on each side, perfect for nighttime reading. The fabric for the custom-made window treatments was purchased from Kirk Brummel, and the trim came from Samuel & Sons. For finishing touches, the wall art was added for a splash of pink. This room was designed to be very sophisticated for two sisters. The intention was that these siblings could have a space that they could mature in. The style and design of this room could last for years to come. *Courtesy of Tony Cacarco Photography.*

Patricia Montalbano of the Montalbano Design Group designed this sophisticated yet whimsical four-year-old girl's room with the intent to carry her from childhood into adolescence. The room features a custom-made, hand-painted bed highlighted by a floral and leaf lattice motif with a seashore medallion. A personalized Queen Anne side chair with a scripted monogram serves as seating for use with the glass door secretary. The wild flower table lamps have pink appliquéd flowers and pearl beads on the shades surrounded by a base of pink metal flowers and a rose beaded and pearl chandelier.

Patricia added an additional custom-made piece, a coordinating chest of drawers in a gingham pattern with floral border and bouquet accents. She hung a pie-crust mirror over this. The floral fabric on the window treatments has also been used on the duvet color and shams, which on the reverse side mimic the pink gingham pattern from the chest of drawers.

If you look closely, you can see the small white birds perched on top of the drapery rods. They are used as tiebacks for the window treatments.

The private bathroom has a green and pink toile fabric shower curtain, which has been enhanced with a pink ribbon and button trim. This curtain pops against the lovely pink floral wall covering. The group added whimsical mermaid hardware as a bit of "jewelry" to the doors of the marble-topped bathroom cabinet.

Not a Literal Princess Look

Shirley Fadden, principal of Wallflowers, designed pink and blue rooms for two girls who wanted a princess feel, but not too literally. Her faux finish covers all the walls. She painted long soft sheers in the corners of the room, using flowers to tie them into the walls. The sheer scallops along the ceiling pull everything together, making the room feel like a tent or canopy. Stars dangle for fun and interest.

Shirley Fadden created a whimsical
wallpaper design for the bathroom.

A Pink Room with a Loft

Terri Crittenden of Susan Fredman Design Group designed this room for a young twin girl. It includes a loft above that connects to a common space shared with her twin. The entire home features a juxtaposition of textures, and this room is no exception. All of the storage, shelving, and architectural details were custom-built on site using reasonably priced materials, including faux-painted plywood. The custom bedding, chair, and bench across from the bed were inspired by the girl's love of pink. *Courtesy of Nick Novelli of Novelli PhotoDesign.*

Pineapple Design was pleased to assist with the décor of a nursery for a new female arrival and with the "graduation" of her sister into "a big girl" room. On the stairwell leading to their new bedrooms, the firm built bookshelves and converted a niche with high narrow windows into a reading nook. It is accessible by a removable ladder. When the parent accompanies their child to the cozy spot for a bedtime story, it establishes a character-building routine. When the girls are older, they can independently maintain the practice because the ladder can be locked in place and they can climb in and out at will. A bench cushion and pillows provide comfort, while the mirrors bolted into the walls increase the size of the platform and give the girls an opportunity to ask "Mirror, mirror on the wall..." *Courtesy of Scott Moore Photography.*

The toddler's bedroom is filled with color and pattern. "We added molding to the angled ceiling; within the resulting frames, we painted delicate branches, singing birds, and flying butterflies. At the intersection of the slanted frames and flat ceiling, we installed sheers and a drapery rail that runs around the base and open edge of the bed. When drawn, the thin panels envelop the sleeping area, which imparts privacy and establishes a unique internal atmosphere." *Courtesy of Scott Moore Photography*.

One of the daughter's favorite activities is having tea with her dollies. A mid-sized dresser sits between her bed and a matching twin setup on the other side of the room. The central dresser has an open shelf and metal containers to help keep her favorite things nearby. She is now agile enough to use a stool to access her bed and moderately high storage shelves in her room, all which are bolted to the wall. *Courtesy of Scott Moore Photography*.

"Tween" Angel

Susan Huckvale Arann of American & International Designs, Inc. found these angelic pillows in an Italian flea market in San Remo, Italy. They inspired this soft, feminine room perfect for the transition from little girl to teenager. The draperies are textured with a lacy design laid over a sheet curtain. They are hung from K. Blair custom designed, gold leaf 3"-thick rods with green and yellow finials. The frame, from Frame Refinishers, is gilded and holds feminine artwork from Frame of Mind. On top of the nightstand from Pier 1 perches a custom water-colored birdcage from the designer's collection. The Ficks Reed daybed makes the most of the space by allowing room for floor activities and can be easily converted into a double-bed.

Pink, White, and Gold

A slatted headboard with angel detailing gives a light, delicate finish to the bed. Choosing uncomplicated, crisp, clean bedding and pairing it with crème and gold gives it a fresh, yet luxurious feel. Mixing and matching patterns with pillows and quilts creates eye-catching contrasts in color and texture, while the bed skirt is a way of adding detail via ruffles.

Pink, white, and gold: A young child sleeps, laughs, and reads in this room created by Rose Abby Design. It is a happy space with nothing built in, so it can easily be updated as she grows. Using white walls is a good way to keep a classic, clean foundation and a perfect backdrop for a transitional space. Acting as a blank canvas, white compliments and contrasts all colors, tones, and textures.

The picture molding, inlaid with damask wallpaper, was used to incorporate detail to the walls, adding a traditional feel to the room. A raspberry and gold color palette for the wallpaper makes a fun choice in a little girl's room.

BOY'S BEDROOMS

Little boys enjoy dinosaurs, trucks, and sharks. Shirley Fadden created a great wall mural of "Jaws" for one.

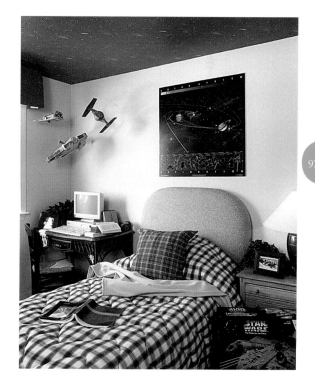

Young Astronomer

Sarah Elizabeth Clinger encourages a child to explore his world in this setting. The night sky on this high ceiling visually lowered this ceiling while lending color and contrast. It also provides an opportunity for learning about the constellations.

The Ultimate
Shared Boy's Room

Hilary Unger of Perianth Interior Design was asked to transform the shared boys' bedroom in an East Side townhouse into a no-holds-barred dream space. Perianth said goodbye to the racecar beds that once filled the room and hello to a Rockwerx Climbing Wall, a punching bag, a mini basketball court, lofts, and more. *Courtesy of Zoe Chan*.

The goals of this project were to create as many activities as possible for the young brothers while keeping the room open and uncluttered. The color palette and materials were chosen on the basis of making the room calm, yet strong. Innovations wallpaper is behind the bookcases; the carpet tile is by Flor. *Courtesy of Zoe Chan.*

Each loft is located in the far corners of the room to allow for floor and game space in the center. The window treatments used Stark fabric and were meant to mimic awnings. Contrasting wood finishes were used to create strength and openness at the same time. *Courtesy of Zoe Chan.*

The loft posts were designed to be thick and solid. Circular cutouts backed in Velcro were created and filled with removable ping pong balls as part of the loft frames. This game kept the children and their siblings busy for hours! *Courtesy of Zoe Chan.*

The room was also designed to contain clutter. The loft spaces were designed to include lots of storage for toys, books, trophies, and, of course, action figures. There is even built-in storage below the windows and beneath the beds. *Courtesy of Zoe Chan.*

Each bed nook has its own wall-mounted plasma TV. Beanbags assist in lounging, and an orange "chalk board" paint on the closet door gives color as well as a place to scribble. A trundle bed under the south loft makes it fun for the occasional sleep-over. *Courtesy of Zoe Chan*.

The light-cerused oak, applied in a herringbone pattern on the underside of the loft, contrasts to the inky-blue stained oak to balance the visual weight. Under-mount puck lights help to create a "nook" feeling for the beds. The bedding is by Bob Williams/Mitchell Gold and DKNY from Bloomingdales. *Courtesy of Zoe Chan*.

Trucks Everywhere!

On the desk, on the dresser, and over the window. Those are real life trucker blades too. Oh, to sleep in a truck! Sandra Clinger of Lifestyle Interior Design drew the concept, cut the headboard and footboard out of MDF, painted the truck in poster colors, attached them to the bed frame and window frame. Then for the coup de grace, the firm installed a set of real truck wiper blades for authenticity! This little boy is ready to go places.

All children love being outside. Shirley Fadden, principal of Wallflowers, created the outdoors scene in this bedroom, along with a great canine companion.

Three's Company

In his renovation of a high-rise apartment, David Sharff Architect, P.C. created a suite for the owner's four young children. Three brothers share this sunny room, designed around built-in beds, desks, and bureaus of natural maple. Sharff designed individual reading nooks in each bunk to make nightly reading fun! Accents like orange Fritz Hansen desk chairs, natural stone knobs, and bright blue walls keep the space playful. The custom wool carpet makes for plenty of happy feet! *Courtesy of Michael J. Lee Photography.*

The sister, being the youngest of the bunch, has her own little hideaway space. Sharff designed white painted built-ins and wainscot paneling. The bed appears to be floating on a custom designed koi pond rug. The custom canopy is draped in silk with glass beads on the façade with a colorful fish print on the inside that only this special little girl enjoys while looking up nestled in her bed. *Courtesy of Michael J. Lee Photography.*

Dots Mark the Spot:
The Shared Boy-Girl
Sibling Bedroom

The goal for this project undertaken by Hilary Unger of Perianth Interior Design was to create a comfortable, happy, and functional bedroom for the boy-girl siblings who share their room while at the same time keeping it non-gender specific. One way of accomplishing this was to utilize multiple colors for the walls. She used a combination of green, teal, purple, and orange to open up the room, make it interesting, and to give it a spacious feel. Perianth added white to the paint to soften the brightness of the colors and thereby maintain a calm feel. The paint is Benjamin Moore #2015-30 Calypso Orange, #534 Crisp Green, #2069-60 Lavender Ice, and #725 Seaside Resort. The bed is by Berg Furniture and the track lighting from Lightolier. *Photo by Michael Falco.*

Storage, play area, floor space, and separate sleeping zones were also key requirements. The desk surface along the window wall is perfect for arts and crafts. In order to create a more spacious layout, the closets along the bed wall of the room were removed. One closet was rebuilt next to the new bed to create a special nook. Other storage elements line the rest of the room, leaving a nice open floor area in the center of the room for play. The STUVA storage armoire and Tobias clear desk chairs are by IKEA. *Photo by Michael Falco.*

Fifty feet of linear shelving provides both a platform for display and easy access for the children's most loved toys. The room has four closets, an armoire, desk cart, and drawers; in other words, there is lots of storage. The wall-mounted shelving is from Knape & Vogt. *Photo by Michael Falco.*

Books give that lived-in feel and provide a personal window inside the residents' interests. *Photo by Michael Falco.*

Trumpets, books, toys, and a blue background are a great combination for eye candy! The paint is Benjamin Moore paint color #725 Seaside Resort, Eggshell finish. *Photo by Michael Falco.*

The detail of this bed highlights the coziness of both spaces. Each child has their own nook surrounded by their own books and toys. The colorful blankets and throw pillows from Gracious Home, polka-dotted sheets, and pillows add to the happy feel of the room. *Photo by Michael Falco.*

This view of the room shows three new closets that were built opposite the bed wall as part of the re-design. The corner closet is large enough to hold a bicycle and a dollhouse. The other two closets house the children's clothing. Mirrors on the face of the doors help reflect the opposite side of the room, as well as allow the toddlers to watch their reflections as they play. Sources: Mirrors by Bed, Bath and Beyond. *Photo by Michael Falco.*

Fraternal twins shared a nursery when the homeowners lived in New York City. The daughter's crib bedding was pink and the boy's was blue. When they moved to the suburbs, each child had their own bedroom. At 3-1/2 years old, the twins had some separation anxiety, although their rooms were down the hall from one another. The parents wanted rooms their son and daughter could grow with. KBK designed a timeless room for each with only the bedding being more age specific.

Any little girl would feel like a princess in this room. Custom bed crown and drapery provide security and intimacy to help with the transition from crib to sleeping in a "big girl" bed. Although she misses sharing a room with her brother, they can play in the "fort-like" canopy of the bed drapery. The ivory linen panels are detailed with grey and white gingham. The bed crown features a monogram with contrasting trim detail. The crown is easily removed as the child grows, leaving a beautifully hand painted iron bed with floral bouquet detailing that a young girl would enjoy. *Courtesy of Wing Wong Memories, LLC.*

A simple mattress ticking fabric "book matched" creates an interesting headboard in this boy's room. Together with the orange lamps, it makes the bedding pop and adds warmth to the space. His mocha walls, orange accents, and the creative use of classic ivory and brown mattress ticking provide timeless details. *Courtesy of Wing Wong Memories, LLC.*

Even children need to just sit in a rocking chair and contemplate their world. Shirley Fadden designed this chair.

The Playroom
THE PLAYROOM

"The pursuit of truth and beauty is a sphere of activity in which we are permitted to remain children all our lives."
— Albert Einstein

ROOMS TO PLAY AND GROW

Courtesy of Scott Moore Photography.

Dedicated Playroom

Joani Stewart-Georgi of Montana Avenue Interiors designed a playroom in the attic of a Cape Cod style house. Her challenge was to create an area for children that would withstand the test of time. Her creation is unique. Any child would know that they were heading somewhere special when they entered this steep and narrow stairway leading to the attic. Safety is mandatory; notice that handrail. The box at the landing made for a perfect fire hydrant created out of wood. *Photo by Grey Crawford.*

The firm used the different floor levels in the attic to define the different parts of the city. The stair landing is a market. A fruit stand complete with baskets full of play fruit and a flower market with pots of play plants stands at the top of the stairs. The closet door was painted to resemble the fruit stand and seller, and the smaller attic door was disguised as Rosey's Flower Mart, complete with Rosy! Notice the flower petals around the AC dial! *Photo by Grey Crawford.*

The largest area became a firehouse with the city painted around the room. A bunk bed was placed in the center of the space for the kids to play or nap. This Hook and Ladder Bunk Bed is a work of art by world renowned artist, Red Grooms. The flag coverlet completes the look. *Photo by Grey Crawford.*

Every surface in the room was completely painted: the ceilings, the beams, and the walls. The AC vent makes for the perfect car grill. Clouds were painted on the ceiling, and a pipe became the perfect flagpole. Large stuffed animals and the toy fire truck driven by a teddy bear in a fireman's cap underscore the theme. *Photo by Grey Crawford.*

The clients wanted to use the room as a place that the kids could have their friends over and host sleep-overs, as well as create a space for the kids to feel comfortable doing whatever they wanted to do safely. The roof-line was very low in one of the areas: difficult for adults, but perfect for young children. Since no kid's room is complete without a window seat, Montana Avenue Interiors created one in keeping with the firehouse theme with the ladder and the firehouse bell. The red and white gingham was the perfect choice for the window seat! *Photo by Grey Crawford.*

This area is stepped up, and the ceiling is so low that only kids fit. The light posts were built out of wood and painted. We wanted a park atmosphere next to the city and the firehouse. The skyline is painted on the back wall; the porthole window becomes a Ferris wheel. The skyline is painted around the perimeter with more light posts and trees. The light posts at the entry of the stairs were built out of wood and painted to seem real. Clouds were painted on the ceiling. The park bench is good for real friends and doll friends. There is a picnic table on the other side of the area for snacks or tea parties. The area rug doubles as a carpet game board! *Photo by Grey Crawford.*

Apartments don't always have room for a children's playroom. Often it has to be incorporated into the family space. The eclectic design of this room created by Marguerite Rodgers reflects the urban melting pot of the city that can be seen from the panoramic views. A modern low sofa showcases the view while providing a comfortable lounge space. A vibrant striped rug adds color to the room and accents the colorful collections that are displayed on the millwork. By mixing vintage pieces, including a set of Dunbar chairs and a modern Flos Arco lamp, this children's den becomes a timeless space where work and play co-habitate. *Courtesy of Peter Aaron/OTTO.*

Marguerite Rodgers designed a play space that doesn't limit a child's imagination. It has ample places to paint, play the guitar, dress-up, or study. "Back Stage," behind the sofa, is an area that houses a table for arts and crafts, a dress-up trunk, and Guitar Hero®. The built-in storage along the interior wall serves as storage for toys, games, and art supplies, with flip down desks that transform the space for homework. *Courtesy of Peter Aaron/OTTO.*

A Star is Born

Pineapple House designers crafted a stage with hardwood floors and full-draw drapery in the playroom, to provide endless possibilities for creativity. A puppet theater is integrated into the back wall. Unfinished attic space with 4' x 8' sub-flooring surrounds two sides of the performance area, imparting the expected "backstage" feel and providing access to the puppet theater. *Courtesy of Scott Moore Photography*.

Costumes are stockpiled in a trunk and used in the children's stage productions while wooden clothespin "people" hang from points on the stationery valance that tops the stage curtains. Each clothespin is painted like a person, using the center separation to distinguish two legs and employing a tassel for hair. *Courtesy of Scott Moore Photography*.

Like many attic spaces, the playroom has a bump-out with dormers. In one alcove, a desk and computer have been placed; in the other, a game table with benches for storage. The game table swivels to allow better access to toys and games that are stashed in the benches. The two alcoves are separated by a television/media center. *Courtesy of Scott Moore Photography*.

The bedroom has an inviting cushioned seat in the window, which encourages the toddler to connect with the outdoors while reading or playing games. The ribbon board holds the little girl's special mementos. *Courtesy of Scott Moore Photography*.

Eco Toddler's Playroom

This project entailed the redesign of a basement area for two toddlers. Sherry Burton Ways of Kreative Ways & Solutions designed the space using eco-friendly wall coverings, upholstered daybeds, and bamboo flooring. *Courtesy of Omar Rafik Lifedepicted Photography.*

This play area also included spaces for play and seating. Sconces accentuate the walls and add additional light. *Courtesy of Omar Rafik Lifedepicted Photography.*

The firm installed a chalkboard for both toddlers to use to learn their ABC's and 1, 2, 3's! A place for learning was essential in the design as well as an area where the children could play. *Courtesy of Omar Rafik Lifedepicted Photography.*

Playroom Paradise for Two Brothers

When this family purchased their new 3,400-square-foot apartment, they wanted to convert one of the extra bedrooms into a playroom for their boys. By removing the corridor partition, Hilary Unger of Perianth Interior Design was able to create an open space for indoor activities, such as climbing, basketball, mini-golf, arts and crafts, and, of course, a toys and games area. On the right side of the room is a climbing wall by Rockwerx and a basketball board by Portable Basketball. The floor was installed with complete soundproofing, and the apartment-wide sound system also filters into this space. *Photo by Michael Falco.*

The basketball lines on the floor were designed and painted by a professional "lines" technician, whose career is actually designing and painting all of the basketball courts for the schools and professional courts throughout the city. The white lines on the pecan floor give it a fresh appearance. The floor mats leaning against the wall are for safety, but also add a nice shot of color to the basketball wall. *Photo by Michael Falco.*

Built-in cabinetry provides the necessary storage space for any playroom; it also allows for easy access to toys and games. The light fixtures above give some much-needed light to the otherwise windowless room. Mini-golf and a rocking horse are just a few of the toys that the children can play with. Flexibility is key, as the games can, of course, be interchangeable. *Photo by Michael Falco.*

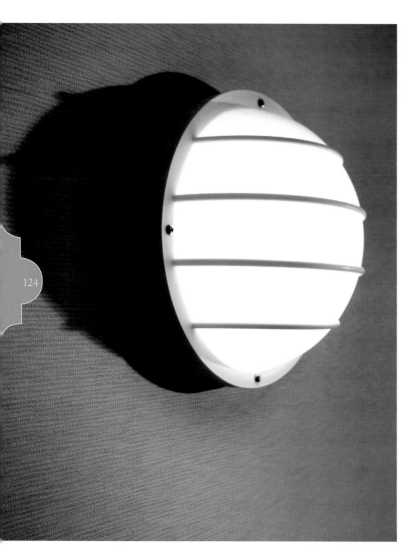

A Progress Lighting wall sconce lights up the wall above the desks (right). Soft-colored peach vinyl wallpaper by Innovations provides texture to a plain wall. The simple flip-down Noruba desks by IKEA for arts and crafts and game playing lend a balance between activity and calmness. *Photo by Michael Falco.*

The goal of this playroom was to design a fun-playing field by bringing outdoor sports indoors. *Photo by Michael Falco.*

Shirley Fadden of Wallflowers believes in encouraging a child's imagination. In the theater scene, she provides a chalkboard for children to draw their own scenery and a trunk filled with dress-up clothes. The window wall gives the feeling of being in a castle.

Shirley's painted indoor and outdoor scenes facilitate the children's creative play.

Tropical Oasis

Vanessa transformed this playroom into a Tropical Forest Oasis with a fun vibe. The soft color palette makes this room peaceful and relaxing while the palm tree and giraffe decals make it come alive. The soft but rugged pink eco-friendly bean bags are perfect for lounging, and the beige chenille fabric on the sofa adds texture. *Courtesy of Vanessa DeLeon Associates.*

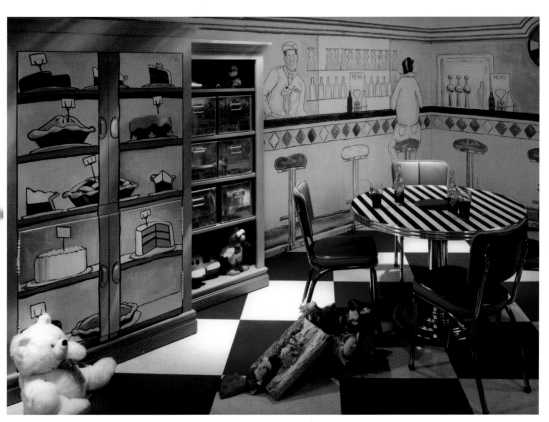

The clients wanted to make a basement/ storage room into a play space for two small children, ages 3 and 5, and a teenager. The room had to work for all ages. Joani Stewart-Georgi of Montana Avenue Interiors transformed the basement from floor to ceiling with 1950s-style table and chairs by Cool Harry Furniture and paintings by Roger Dolin/Mural Environments. Even Elvis is in the room — he's sipping a soda at the soda fountain! The armoire looks like a glass refrigerator for pies and cakes, but in reality hides the TV and has plenty of storage space inside. The open part of the unit is filled with metal boxes to organize the toys. *Photo by Douglas Hill.*

Even the name of the diner is painted to look like it is outside the window. The painted booths replicate the real chairs in the room. Is that Fonzie in the booth? What about the Martian? Notice the robot by the first booth — is he painted or real? *Photo by Douglas Hill.*

The other side of the playroom contains video games and a music machine. The spaceship crashed into the wall. Kids of all ages love this space. There is something for everyone! What a great place for a party! *Photo by Douglas Hill.*

Room with a View

Marguerite Rodgers believes in surrounding yourself with things that make you happy, such as dark brown walls with colorful accents like a box of chocolate. This playful escape, whether getting lost in a good book or playing with dolls, invites you to let your imagination run wild. The daybed functions as both a sofa to hang out on with friends and a hidden trundle bed for slumber parties. The vintage cabinet, painted with a fantasy landscape, allows for ample storage space as well the display of books and art projects. The overall neutral palette of the space will stand the test of time as this little girl grows up — a room with a view like this never goes out of style. *Courtesy of Peter Aaron/OTTO.*

In this activity room for a boy, Pineapple House Interior Design (Stephen Pararo, Zach Azpeitia, Nikki Bachrach, and Mollie Chalk Monkaitis) uses multiple green Lego-base platforms to make two large horizontal areas for constructing and displaying LEGO® creations. The bricks vary in size, but they all will fit on the green platforms. To keep them from being swallowed at the baby or toddler stage, the child at ages one to five starts building with the largest blocks and advances to smaller bricks as they get older. *Courtesy of Scott Moore Photography.*

One of the Lego "walls" is actually a sliding barn door for a closet, which serves as the room's transformable hiding place. For the child's camping experience, it is currently tented. Future plans are for it to be a club house and, later, a reading library. *Courtesy of Scott Moore Photography.*

The activity room has two armoires that are used for storage. In the unit on the right, there is a "secret" passageway into the toddler's bedroom (à la *The Chronicles of Narnia*). The passage connects two closets. Hanging clothing on both sides "blocks" the opening from being noticed by the unsuspecting eye. *Courtesy of Scott Moore Photography.*

The two armoires significantly increase storage capabilities, as they can house anything from clothing to the largest of games and toys. *Courtesy of Scott Moore Photography.*

The console under the flat screen TV is filled with easy to reach drawers that help the child keep smaller items easily accessible and organized. *Courtesy of Scott Moore Photography*.

Several trunks with safety-closing lids offer storage for bulky items. *Courtesy of Scott Moore Photography.*

137

American & International Designs, Inc.

Susan Huckvale Arann
1110 South Avenue, Suite 2
Staten Island, New York 10314
designamericanyc@aol.com

Susan says, "I'm a green, environmentally conscious designer with a love for color and a flair for international elements. I combine color, scale, and texture in each space; I often find inspiration in nature. Design is about layering colors, finding interesting finishes, and giving a space dimension. My clients have a vision for their space and over the past thirty years I've loved working with them to realize their design dreams. I've been recognized with awards, noted for my work with color, and involved with color forecasting in the design industry. I enjoy presenting at *Architectural Digest* shows and other industry events.

"My involvement with the Window Covering Association, both as a member and a judge, makes me an expert in window fashions while my passion for fashion drives my keen interest in pop art. As past president of the New York City chapter of ASID, I encourage a respect for certification in the field. Project problems are minimized when you use an experienced, certified professional. In the end, my satisfied clients speak for me: 'They did it perfectly. I honestly feel like I couldn't have asked for a better job. I tried to express to Susan what style I was looking for. I think she understood it right off of the bat. Susan helped me with color 100%. She knew what colors to match to the wallpaper and furniture and a lot of the colors ... I never would have thought of.'"

CasaPosh

PO Box 49078
Austin, Texas 78765
megan@casaposh.com

CasaPosh is a small interior design firm in the San Antonio/Austin area that has completed a wide range of projects in our seven-plus years in business. A design firm for all styles, "we help the client understand their aesthetic preferences and build spaces that are not only stylish but also personalized. We believe that at the end of the day, your space should speak volumes about who you are and the journey you have taken. Combining an unexpected mix of textures with classic color palettes and unique furnishings, we create timeless spaces that grow with our clients.

"Our goal is to provide you with a living design plan, where interchangeable elements accommodate future needs and growing families. We balance function and aesthetics, leaving you with a space that meets your needs in the most stylish way possible."

139

David Sharff
Architect, P.C.

67 West Street
Medfield, Massachusetts 02052
david@davidsharffarchitect.com

Building or transforming your home should be a collaborative process and deliver a discerning design solution tailored to your needs. Since 1995, David Sharff Architect, P.C., has been implementing this approach in partnership with our clients to deliver award-winning designs for new homes, whole house renovations, additions, and interiors. Through the thoughtful integration of beauty and function, form, space, and material, the firm instills the feeling that while fresh, beautiful, new, antique, or modern..."this feels like it has been here forever."

An early interest in art, history, and construction led David Sharff into the field of architecture. David launched his practice with a focus on detail-oriented residential design and home renovation. Today, his award-winning firm's designs can be seen enhancing neighborhoods throughout New England.

David Sharff Architect designed projects have been featured in *Design New England* and *New England Home* magazines, as well as *Boston Globe Magazine*, and on Discovery Home Channel's *Houselift*, ABC's *Extreme Makeover: Home Edition*, and HGTV's *Bang for your Buck*. Its extensive experience in residential architecture and interiors results in a sensitive integration of new and old. David Sharff Architect, P.C. offers a client-focused, relationship-driven approach to working with you to achieve architectural excellence, thoughtful transformations, and sensible designs based on how you live and use your home.

dBk Interiors Inc.

206 Sussex Road
Washington Township,
New Jersey 07676
www.DBKInteriors.com
DBKInteriors@verizon.net

dBk Interiors Incorporated is comprised of a style and expertise that is a distinctive combination of a Mother's and Daughter's experiences, education, and hard work. Their formal education in both art and interior design offers an individual perspective, which often results in a unique project solution.

The company strives to design for the end user, listening to and guiding the homeowner to a mutually pleasing design. Never attempting to put a recognizable stamp on their projects, their work truly reflects the taste and personality of the client. The result is an exceptional and livable space pleasing to all involved esthetically and practically.

After fifteen years of successful design work, they say, "We are pleased with the diversity of our portfolio. We present it to you on our web pages, for your consideration on your next project. Be the project large or small, residential or commercial, in state or beyond, our commitment to your project remains. Our designs are one of a kind and inspire 'Room Envy.'

"Many of our projects have been chosen for publication; some have won awards. Our biggest successes, however, are our long and fulfilling relationships with our happy clients."

Design Concepts/ Interiors, LLC

Phyllis Harbinger
8 Devonshire Court
Cortlandt Manor, New York 10567
Phyllis@dcistudio.com

Phyllis Harbinger, ASID, is a professional interior designer and certified Feng Shui consultant. She is the founder of Design Concepts/Interiors, LLC and has been running the boutique luxury design firm since 1993. Phyllis and her team work on a myriad of projects, including high-rise apartments at the Ritz and Trump Plaza as well as serving the affluent in tony locales such as Purchase and Kings Point, New York.

Her style is eclectic, mixing unique finds with transitional elements for a blended and timeless aesthetic. Phyllis has been featured as the winning designer on HGTV's hit show *Designer's Challenge* and she also appeared as a guest judge on HGTV's *Battle on the Block*. She is listed on Top10ofNewYork.com as a top interior designer and is also a member of Cambridge's Who's Who.

Evelyn Benatar

New York Interior Design
Evelyn@NYinteriordesign.com

Evelyn Benatar is a professional interior designer with over fifteen years of experience. New York Interior Design offers a complete range of services from inception to completion, as well as consultations. Evelyn focuses on both residential and commercial spaces mostly in Manhattan, Westchester, and the North Shore of Long Island.

Over the years, Evelyn has developed a style that is refined yet edgy. Symmetry is balanced with the unexpected. Her projects are always clean, refreshing, and polished. Evelyn's ability to draw on an encyclopedic knowledge of ideas makes overcoming design challenges easy. Supporting her is a coterie of highly skilled craftsmen, fully capable of molding dreams into reality. Focusing on the synthesis of light and color enables Evelyn to transform a home into an eminently livable show place. With an intimate knowledge of showrooms, galleries, and resources, Evelyn can enhance the vision of any client she collaborates with. Her inspiring work has been published in numerous interior design publications.

A graduate of The New York School of Interior Design and The Fashion Institute of Technology (cum laude), Evelyn is known for an uncompromising ability to create rooms that are imbued with elegance and originality, always managing to reflect the client's personal taste. She is known for her modern transitional style using the surprise of antiques and avant-garde elements; yet she is equally at home with classic tastes, rendering rooms that are both timeless and timely.

Jen Meyer Interiors

Jennifer Meyer
Short Hills, New Jersey 07078
www.JenMeyerInteriors.com

A fundamental theme for Jen Meyer Interiors is that "every room should have an unexpected element." The unexpected element can be found in use of color, placement of art, or a great family heirloom. A little bit of humor can also add life to a room. It's important that a room is not static, which can occur with an overemphasis on matching. Colors, as well as small sculptures, photos, or art, can bring a smile to one's face. This approach helps a room transcend time.

Jen Meyer Interiors was founded in 2009. Prior to opening her own design firm, Jennifer spent twenty years specializing in corporate design, art, and, more recently, residential. She had established a worldwide art collection for a leading fund management corporation, as well as consulting on private collections. Interior design is a second career for her. She graduated with a degree in Economics and spent several years as a financial analyst before pursuing a degree in interior design in New York City.

KBK Interior Design

Kingsley Belcher Knauss, ASID
205 Benson Place
Westfield, New Jersey 07090
info@kbkinteriordesign.com

Kingsley says, "I feel that design should reflect the client's personality and have the longevity to stand the test of time and passage of design trends. It is my job as the designer to hone in on a client's desires and help them organize and edit their aesthetic. Whimsy and trendsetting elements are added based on the temperament of the client and their sense of style. I often refer to myself as a 'design librarian.' The fabrics, finishes, millwork, and furnishings are the reference materials that I provide to build the character of the space linking both architectural and interior elements. If a space has good bones, then the client's personality and priorities can be built upon over time when tastes may change.

"Children's tastes change as quickly as they grow. My preference when designing for a child is to select less juvenile elements that can evolve as the child grows and let their toys and day-to-day items reflect their age. Although I have done plenty of high-end custom bunk beds and bed canopies, I often point out to the client that a child will only like this until a certain age. For example, does the majority of the budget go into custom cabinets to provide storage and future study needs or into soft treatments like custom bedding and window treatments to fulfill the desired concept or child fantasy? It is important to setup design concepts that help the client prioritize where they want to spend their money and the longevity of a particular design element."

In addition to receiving design awards and being featured in coffee table and magazine publications, the firm's timeless interior design has been featured on NBC's *Housesmart* television program.

Katie Reynolds, RID

Lilli Design LLC
5914 Richmond
Dallas, Texas 75206
katie@lilli-design.com

A Texas-based interior designer with a passion for creating beautiful and inviting children's rooms, Katie Reynolds spent a decade in the luxury hotel design industry working for several of the most well known international design firms. Over the years she has spent time traveling to far-flung locations around the globe, and it was her experiences in some of the most glamorous and lavish hotels that gave her a desire to create the same feel in unique and luxurious nurseries for her clients.

Katie says, "I am not one for themes or characters; rather I strive to evoke a feeling of warmth, comfort, and elegance in spaces that can grow with the child. Using handmade and found objects is my specialty, and I love to play with pattern and texture. As a mother to two young children, I also am very well versed in safety and practicality and believe that beauty and luxury are not exclusive of function. The rooms that I create are personalized gems that each of my clients can enjoy creating many blessed memories in for years to come."

Kreative Ways & Solutions, LlC (KWS)

Sherry Burton Ways
1341 H. Street N.E., Suite 201
Washington, DC 20002
interiors@kreativeways.com
www.kreativeways.com

In 2004, Sherry Burton Ways transformed her life from a national policy expert with the Federal Government to one that transforms people's lives through their homes. Realizing a knack for decorating personal spaces, she studied interior design and expanded her personal awareness.

Sherry's work focuses on designing interiors that promote the health and well-being for both the residential and commercial clientele. Enthusiastic about designing interiors using color therapy, Feng Shui, and eco-friendly design, she assists her clients to understand what is blocking them in their lives by looking at the spaces they occupy and the color they surround themselves with.

Sherry's design work has been featured in the DC, Virginia, and Maryland-based *Home & Design Magazine*, *DC Luxury Magazine*, the *Washington Post*, and the *Washington Examiner*, as well as on WUSA Channel 9 News (Washington, DC), to name a few. She is the Senior Design Editor for *How We Live Magazine*.

Lifestyle Interior Design

Sandra Elizabeth Clinger
lifestyle@ecentral.com

Sandra says, "As the somber, solemn president of Lifestyle Interior Design, an international interior design and model home merchandising firm, I have had lighthearted times designing children's rooms in playful, color-driven materials while seriously developing interactive, engaging child-to-child and child-to-adult layouts. I consult with my custom home clients and/or their builders, developing comforting and amusing specifications, shopping and purchasing therapy (my therapy!), and then overseeing final installations. The good-natured, lively experience of children's rooms offers me a tiny window of opportunity for mischief — mine, not theirs.

"My more fundamental interior design work is featured in over fifty publications, including *Ultimate Decorating and Cabin Style* by Publications International and *Today's Historic Interiors* by Schiffer Publishing. I have been honored as the first-place recipient of numerous design awards, including the ASID IDA Award with Special Recognition for Aging in Place, the CARE Award for Historic Preservation, the coveted national ASID Design Specialty Award for Historic Preservation, and the CH&L Home of the Year Award. My work is the subject of two distinct episodes on HGTV. Look for replays in *Renovation Generation*."

Marguerite Rodgers
Interior Design

Marguerite Rodgers
2131 North American St.
Philadelphia, Pennsylvania 19122
www.mrodgersltd.com

Every interior design commission represents a chance to create something that never existed before: an opportunity to step inside a client's dreams and fashion a new world. Since 1980, Marguerite Rodgers has been doing just that — listening well, imagining out loud, and forging unforgettable spaces that speak for and of the client. Classic symmetry is at work in the firm's designs, as are clean lines, an accommodating scale, and a multifaceted vocabulary of materials, textures, and finishes. Beauty and serenity are finally paramount. Built on long-term relationships and an overall desire to get things just right, Marguerite Rodgers Interior Design, in its fourth decade, holds an enduring reputation as a firm that fully respects its clients and successfully exceeds expectations.

The International Interior Design Association (IIDA) recently awarded Marguerite Rodgers its Best Interior Design Award for 2011.

Marsh & Clark Design

Stephanie Marsh Fillbrandt
2721 Bush Street
San Francisco, California 94115
www.marshandclark.com

Since 2004, Stephanie's award-winning residential and commercial interior design firm, Marsh & Clark, has created exquisite interiors that are as comfortable as they are inviting. Marsh & Clark's portfolio includes boutique hotels and residential projects scattered throughout the West.

California-born and Wyoming-bred, Stephanie's philosophy is one of "relaxed sophistication." With an extensive knowledge of materials, craftsmanship, and architecture, her broad use of luxurious, sustainable materials, fine craftsmanship, and custom-design elements has become hallmarks of her firm's work.

Stephanie earned her BA in International Business from the University of California at Davis and studied Interior Architecture and Design at the University of California at Berkeley.

A trusted voice on achieving a discerning elegance based in comfort and livability, Marsh & Clark's work has been featured in *Travel + Leisure*, *House Beautiful*, and *USA Today*. The firm was also selected for the 2009 and 2010 San Francisco Decorator's Showcase.

Montalbano Design Group

Patricia A. Montalbano
31 Morningside Circle
Little Falls, New Jersey 07424
montdsgngrp@aol.com

Patricia Montalbano, ASID, specializes in interiors that exhibit warmth and charm while remaining fully attentive to the demands of the client's lifestyles. She is the owner of the Montalbano Design Group, Inc., a full-service interior design firm with thirty years of experience. Its staff includes qualified interior designers and administrative personnel, as well as a registered architect. Montalbano Design Group specializes in a complete range of residential interiors, including kitchens and bathrooms, from design concept to completion.

Long fascinated by history and cultural studies, and possessing an exquisite color sense, Ms. Montalbano brings an educated eye to projects that cover a range of styles and eras. She is a professional member of ASID and is National Council for Interior Design Qualification (NCIDQ) certified. She is also licensed in the state of Florida, certified in the state of New Jersey, and has overseen many long-distance projects, including residences in North Carolina, Florida, and the Outer Banks. She is past president of the New Jersey Chapter of ASID.

Ms. Montalbano has been honored with the NJ/ASID Medalist award, which is bestowed for distinguished service to the chapter and to the design profession. Her firm has won multiple design excellence awards for both commercial and residential projects and her work has been widely published in book form, as well as in numerous local and national publications.

Montana Avenue Interiors

Joani Stewart
4333 Admiralty Way
Marina del Rey, California 90292
joanistewart@montanaaveinteriors.com

152

Joani says, "Interior design has always been my passion. I attended the UCLA Interior Design Program and was proud to be selected to intern with the late, great Tony Duquette. Once out of school, I worked with a few very well-known, successful, and talented designers. In 1994, I established Montana Avenue Interiors on the very trendy Montana Avenue in Santa Monica. I saw so many kids in strollers and moms walking up and down the street, I knew that was where I wanted to build my business. I started my design studio designing kids rooms ... my logo became 'Interior Design with Kids in Mind.' I love doing nurseries and kids rooms (although we do much more than that!) because of the absolute creativity involved and the excitement of everyone involved.

"I have been very fortunate to be interviewed on television for *Beautiful Homes and Great Estates*, *Find!*, and several TV news broadcast segments dedicated to interior design. I have been published in over thirty periodicals over the years, gotten a few cover stories, and have been lucky enough to have been published in many design books, including *Creating Your Dream Bedroom* (with our project on the cover!), *Best of Today's Interior Design*, and *Designer Showcase – Interior Design at its Best*. Design and art are my passion and they go hand-in-hand. I can't do one without the other. I feel collaboration between homeowner and the designer is the key to great design."

Perianth Interior Design
Buy My Eye® Interior
Design Services at a Glance

Hilary Unger, ASID Principal
204 West 84th Street, 3rd Floor
New York, New York 10024
www.perianth.com
www.buymyeye.net
maca@perianth.com

Hilary says, "My work as an interior designer has always been meaningful to me. It gives me the opportunity to improve people's surroundings, which ultimately improves their quality of life. Since I was young, I've always been impacted by my physical environment with regard to light, organization, and the general feel of the space around me. When things are in order, there is a peacefulness that follows. Chaos and disorder can create stress. I'm acutely aware that our surroundings provoke various emotions, and I bear that in mind when I work with my clients.

"In all of my designs, my goal is to address my clients' most needed 'functions' first, and as such, we begin with the basics: What will the space be used for? Once functionality is addressed, we then make the environment beautiful, incorporating color, fabrics, and textures. My philosophy is that our design plan must translate visually into what the client is hoping to convey, and it's my job to make their wishes come true (in the most tasteful way!).

"When I first meet with a client, I immediately get a sense of them, their aesthetic, and their ideal physical environment. An important element I'm always careful to bear in mind is that the design is not about me — it is about the client and what they want, what is important to them, and how they want to live. I just bring my level of expertise to whatever look is desired.

"Regardless of our income level and the square footage we have to work with, we all want to live in a peaceful, functional, wonderful home. With my two companies, Perianth Interior Design and Buy My Eye, I aim to help people attain their level of comfort and create beauty at the same time. With fifteen years of experience, I stand by my track record of delivering on that promise."

Pineapple House
Interior Design

Stephen Pararo, Zach Azpeitia, Nikki
Bachrach, and Mollie Chalk Monkaitis
190 Ottley Drive, Atlanta, Georgia
info@pineapplehouse.com
www.pineapplehouse.com

154

Pineapple House designers enjoy decorating for youngsters. Since, by necessity, minors spend years being directed and controlled, the firm makes sure their principal personal space — their bedroom — is safe and engaging. The firm's designers want the child's independence, imagination, and individuality nurtured while they are free from supervision.

The firm's designers point out, "Visual stimulation is our primary objective with infant decor. As babies become toddlers, we introduce design elements to fuel creativity and perpetuate good habits. For example, we make sure children can reach their belongings and 'take out' and 'clean up' by themselves.

"Males and females interact differently with their surroundings. Girl toddlers tend to set up family structures and act out scenarios. This makes props, costumes, and stages wonderful resources. Boys are drawn to mobility, gadgets, sounds, and construction. Television and computers will eventually fascinate both boys and girls, so desks, monitors, and play stations are considered in every scheme. Child-friendly design doesn't have to look juvenile. In kitchens, low shelving and baskets provide little ones with access to their own plates, utensils, and personal items — while being stylish."

Pineapple House Interior Design is a full-service firm whose award-winning designers hold degrees in either interior design or architecture. Its projects have appeared in coffee table books, textbooks, hundreds of magazines, and on nine television networks.

Rose Abby Design

info@roseabbydesign.com
www.roseabbydesign.com

"I have been driven by two significant interests in my life: my enduring passion for interior design and my study of psychology. My design process encompasses primary, interrelated phases of discovery that enables deep, personal understanding of space. A strong collaboration between client and designer is paramount to the process and allows for a translation of the client's experiences into design elements such as color, light, furnishings, materials, and space utilization.

"Every interior has a functional purpose; this allows for ease and maximization of utility, but meaningful design must have a personality. It is the subconscious of a space that most resonates in a successful design, and it is my goal to transpose a client into the space, sometimes fusing multiple personalities and styles in a single project. As a designer it is important for me to transcend utility and visual appeal by delivering a visceral reaction that has the ability to evoke love, joy, tenderness, safety, relaxation, confidence, and prestige — not only to those that own/inhabit the space, but also to those that come into contact with it. I consider design a work of art; it is subjective and meaningful, and transcends emotion and provides an outlet for self-expression. Each design is a personal experience, and having a client allow me into their space is something I value highly."

Sissy + Marley

A Beautiful Beginning
hello@sissyandmarley.com
www.sissyandmarley.com

As expectant mothers, we were determined to balance our successful careers, busy social calendars, and tendencies for perfectionism, all while making room for baby. And so Sissy + Marley, a New York City-based boutique baby planner and concierge service, was born.

At Sissy + Marley, we know that children are affected by their surroundings and stimulated by color, texture, light, and sound. We are passionate about design and creating inspired children's spaces that foster growth and exploration. Our goal is always to create stylish spaces for sleep and play that are as beautiful as they are functional. The firm's work has been featured in *Trad Home*, *Ohdeedoh*, *Nursery Notations*, and on blogs around the world.

Susan Fredman Design Group

350 W. Erie
Chicago, Illinois 60654
info@susanfredman.com
www.susanfredman.com

Established in 1975, the Susan Fredman Design Group is an award-winning residential and commercial interior design firm. With more than fifteen designers, it is one of the largest residential design firms in the country; they have earned a national reputation and established full-service offices in downtown Chicago, Michigan's Harbor Country, and Milwaukee. They approach each project as a unique collaborative process, committed to exchanging ideas and developing a synergistic relationship between client, designer, and environment. They work in a variety of styles, on projects both large and small, all around the country, including urban lofts, family homesteads, and more. Every member of Susan Fredman Design Group is devoted to meeting their clients' needs and providing a unique solution for each environment.

The recipient of numerous awards and honors, the firm is widely recognized as a leader in the Chicago design community and beyond, and their work has garnered the attention of the media, including *Traditional Home*, *Chicago Tribune*, *Chicago* magazine, *Chicago Home + Garden*, *LUXE Interiors + Design*, *Chicago Social*, *Chicago Social Interiors*, HGTV, Fox-TV, and NBC-TV, among others.

In 2000, Susan Fredman founded Designs for Dignity, a non-profit organization that transforms the existing spaces of non-profits through pro bono design services and in-kind donations. To learn more about Designs for Dignity, visit their website at www.designsfordignity.com.

Vanessa DeLeon
Associates

Vanessa DeLeon
934 1/2 River Road
Edgewater, New Jersey 07020

One Little West 12th Street
New York, New York 10014
info@vanessadeleon.com

Vanessa says, "Along with my family history of creative genes and encouragement, I knew I had a place in the arts; that art would be design/architecture. I have found myself creating a new look and feel that takes on streamline minimalism, with a sharp eye for glamorous details, which resulted in my signature style 'Glamilistic.' I was able to grow and further develop my style and designs via many genres of the design world, including: high-end residential homes, commercial venues, and hospitality facilities.

"You can catch me on HGTV, the Food Channel Network, and *Restaurant Impossible*, as well as in publications such as *New York Spaces*, *Design NJ*, *Latina Magazine*, and *Cosmopolitan*. In addition to being Interior Design/Architecture Editor for *SOMA Magazine*, I have been featured in numerous design books published by Schiffer."